God, I love you and I thank you for life. It has been an adventure beyond my dreams. It has been an amazing gift with ongoing surprises. The journey became more awesome when my relationship and bond with you became unbreakable. I am so blessed because of you. Thank you for health, strength, family, joy, love, peace, happiness, understanding, clarity, five senses and your Universe. I asked in your name and I received.

THE JOURNEY OF FAITH

By

Tiffany N. Alston

Editor: Donna Bosink

Cover Concept: Tiffany N. Alston

Cover Design: Brittany J. Jackson

Published by G Publishing, LLC

Library of Congress Control Number: 2020909931

ISBN: 978-1-7340865-3-9

Printed in the United States of America

Contents

DEDICATIONS

THE JOURNEY OF FAITH

I have learned in this life that you must live before you die inside. God, I thank you for helping me understand your laws and what my true gifts are in life.

In this next chapter in life, I will base my decisions on everything I have learned since I've been on this earth. I am so grateful you have given me clarity in this life.

I will continue spreading your greatness and building your

Kingdom. I will let no one separate me from your love. I already know that you will supply my every need as you have always done. You have been AMAZING. Your presence makes my heart feel warm like no one else ever could. I am so grateful for my relationship with you. I will always have faith because you have shown me that the impossible is possible. Thank you! I love you God! It feels so great to be alive!

To my Husband Donald: This life with you has been a ride or die. I could never replace you or our love or friendship. The way we met was divine. Thank you for loving me the way you do. Your love, trust and understanding has helped me become the woman I am today. We are both living out our vows to the fullest, never giving up on one another and being forgiving to each other and always putting the pieces back together no matter how broken they are. Til death do us part, I am here. As I look back at our lives I smile because if we knew then what we know now, our choice to be together would still be the same. I am looking forward to sharing our story with many others in this life, and also creating a new story as we live our best lives now and teach others who are willing to learn to make wise choices for their lives. Thanks for being a wonderful husband and best friend.

My three sons Christopher, Christian, and Cameron: My life has never had a dull moment! I'm so thankful that God has blessed me with you. You gave me and your dad a family. It has been an awesome challenging experience trying to mold you and prepare you for the real world while you're under my wings. This book is for you and many others in the world as you go through your journeys of life.

I pray that all three of you remain close and have each others back. Encourage one another to live a good positive life. When one is down lift the other up even if it's through prayer. Remember: God First Always. Never forget any of the things I have taught you. If life gets hard remember to create your own reality. Read the bible and books that your father and I have written. When you get older study laws of attraction. Always be open minded and trust your intuitions. This life can be whatever you want it to be as long as you make wise choices. Be brave, humble, loving, respectful, and kind. Remember that what you put out in this life is what you will get back. You reap what you sow; it's a law. Smile daily and know and understand that happiness is inside of you.

To my mother Jeanette Lenoir: Thank you for never giving up. You are one of the strongest women I have ever met in this life. As a young child I watched you go through so much heartache and pain but you always remained so loving to everyone in the world and with forgiveness in your heart. Through the good times and bad times I watched you hold on to God's unchanging hand. I watched you put your faith and trust 100% in God. I heard you call on Jesus because you believed in Him. No matter what happened in your life or how many setbacks you still remain blessed. Thank you for paving the way for me to have remarkable faith in this life. I saw you praying and trusting God so this allowed me to know what our Creator of the heavens and earth was capable of. One of the best gifts in my life is having you as a role model as a mom. The struggle was real while my brother and I were young but you never gave up and now you get to reap what you sowed during all those tough days we had.

Thank you, God, for seeing my mom through all her trials. You worked everything out in her favor because she trusted you. The joy is so real just to see her have peace.

To my dad, Robert Lenoir: I'm so blessed to have you. You have raised me and built my mind to be strong and never intimidated. You taught me good work ethics, how to respect other people in the world, managing money skills, and how to be successful honestly. You have told me everything that I need in this life to survive. Because of you I am a leader with many managing skills. I was often angry because you didn't hand me things on a silver platter but I now thank you because this only made me stronger and taught me not to depend on anyone but God in this life. Thanks for instilling awareness in my mind when I was so naive about all the things that were going on around me.

To my brother, Robert Lenoir III: You are my only sibling. You have been wonderful and have always had my back. Thank you for allowing me to be like a second mom to you as we were growing up. I can't explain in words how blessed I was to get you in this life for a brother. You have never left me behind and I will always do the same for you and your family throughout this life. The times when I was down you reached back for me with loving arms and a helping hand and I will never forget this. I'm so grateful. "Dimples" - Bro, only you and I know what that means. I thank God for blessing you with your amazing wife Dorisha. Dorisha, you have been the sister-in-law that everyone should want. I'm so proud of you and my brother and the fact that you trust God and you have created a life of goodness for family by staying focused. Thanks for being my sis. Love you both.

My father- and mother-in-law Donald and Wonda Alston: You have inspired me to pull out my inner strength and grow spiritually stronger. I truly appreciate the support you have given our family with our children over the years. You have been such loving grandparents to my children. Your son has been one of the greatest blessings of my life.

Donna Bosink: You have been such a great friend, and my editor. You are also one of God's gifts to me. We are so different but we connect in so many ways. We can trust and talk about things that others would never enjoy. We both appreciate the important things in life. You are a beautiful soul with a love for the earth and people in the world that is amazing and inspiring to me. Thanks for being a part of my family's life and sharing amazing memories and making special moments full of laughter and joy. It's been so great to have you in my life. Cheers to infinity and beyond!

Deanetris Armstrong: You were truly a Godsend. I can't even begin to express what you have done for my family. I thank you for being one of the most AWESOME caring teachers I have ever met. You have loved my children and many others as if they were your own. You have been a counselor, protector, doctor, and a mentor. Hats off to you for being so loving and passionate and going beyond the call of duty to help families. You helped give us peace of mind as we struggled with our children throughout school. You push them to be the best they could be. We love you and are forever grateful.

ACKNOWLEDGEMENTS

Nysean Crofton, Michelle Gray, Aaron Hickmon, LaShonda Jack, Yaka Watson, Annette Marks, LyTania Tolbert, Alieen Taylor-Spence, Mary Whitehead, Carlos Benton, Rhonda Benton: I thank God for having you as my family, neighbors and lifetime friends. You are all a true example of what good hearted people should be.

I thank you for showing up in my family's life and on our doorstep multiple times to give a helping hand, word of encouragement, smile, food, clothes, gifts, and whatever we needed. You have all been so AWESOME. I love you all and appreciate you more than words can say.

INTRODUCTION

Thank you God for blessing me and anyone that is reading this with the gift of life. I pray that this book blesses generations.

I am a 39 year old working mother of 3 children and the spouse of a wonderful man of God who has been diagnosed with end-stage kidney failure and is currently on dialysis. God, I am thanking you in advance that my husband Donald C. Alston Jr. is healed by your stripes.

I Am healthy

I Am wealthy

I Am beautiful

I Am grateful

I Am bold

I Am confident

I Am smart

I Am thankful.

No matter what life presents us with, we must still keep pressing forward to be the best version of ourselves. We all have a purpose on the earth and everything in our life happens for a reason.

Throughout my journey of faith I began to look at challenges as experiences. I found a way to find positivity in everything that was thrown my way. I learned that we must all expect the unexpected from another human being. Because we are all human, we all make mistakes.

God our Creator is who we can all trust. Be thankful for all the people who are put in our lives and learn from one another.

We are all on this earth for only a limited amount of time. How are you spending yours?

What goodness are you putting

out in to the earth? Have material possessions consumed your life and thoughts or is peace overcoming you because you know what is important?

CHAPTER 1

Prayer Changes Things

Pause and take three slow deep breaths.

The average person spends more time worrying about the weight of the world rather than being thankful for life which could end at any second or moment of the day or night.

People of the world today are having anxiety and depression levels higher than ever. We have the power to control this ourselves if we have knowledge and understanding of who we are and what we are capable of when we are focused and in alignment. Medications and surgeries are not always needed for healing. If your mind is sick, so can your thoughts and body be. It all starts with who you surround yourself with and what you are eating daily. The healthier you eat, the clearer your thoughts are and the more positive your reactions are to negative situations.

As young children most of us were taught to eat three meals a day - breakfast, lunch and dinner, with snacks in between. We were taught to follow a food pyramid with a certain amount of servings a day that our body needs to maintain to be healthy. As I did research and experienced my husband's near-death health crisis (which is revealed in the book *I Am Healed Walking in Faith*), I realize most of us are overeating. People think it's so expensive to eat healthy but it's really not, once you're eating to survive and not for pleasure. We really don't need a lot of food to survive. We mainly need water and non-GMO fruits and vegetables.

Drinking water first thing in the morning when we wake up can help rehydrate, increase alertness, fuel your brain, strengthen your immune system, remove toxins, jump-start metabolism, reinforce weight loss, improve skin and hair growth, and prevent kidney stones and bladder infections. People say breakfast is the most important meal of the day. But when you wake up in the morning your body has a hard time processing bacon, eggs, sausage, chicken and waffles etc. After we have had our morning water, a few hours later fruit is great for breakfast.

Our bodies know exactly how to store fruit in the morning and will not be overworked breaking it down. All of our bodies are different, so each individual should base diet and exercising on one's own body structure and family history to maintain health.

This nutrition-based approach has made a world of difference in our family.

My husband and I and others realized since birth that my oldest son was extra active and hyper. The first night that he was in the world, even though I had just given birth, the nurses refused to keep him in the nursery with all the other babies at the hospital. They brought him back to my room and said, "Ma'am, I'm sorry you have to keep him in your room. He is disturbing all the other babies." They stated that he was going to be a really active child and I might have problems when he goes to school.

When I took my newborn baby home the next day, I was exhausted from a long labor and had no help from the staff at the hospital so I could not rest before coming home as a new mother.

By the time my child was six months he was doing extra. As people would say, he was getting out of the way for the next one. He was shaking the crib, climbing out and walking at 8 months. It was almost as if he had been here before. I took him to doctor visits frequently but I didn't want him to be diagnosed with Attention Deficit Hyperactivity Disorder (ADHD) because I felt he was too young. So we just kept a close eye on him and observed his daily behaviors. He always seemed to be bouncing off the walls (and some days he literally was) and rolling around on the floor.

As he entered his toddler stage I noticed he never could sit down for long periods of time. By the time he was around 6, I noticed as we ate dinner I would have to constantly remind him to sit down in the chair and not stand in it as we ate. I knew it was abnormal because by this time I was a mother of two children.

My second son, who was 3 years younger, had no problem sitting through dinner with no reminders.

As my oldest son entered kindergarten he had multiple issues with behavior. He was giving the teachers difficulty. He even made them, and me, shed tears. He would destroy things in the classroom; he did not respect adults; he used bad language; he put his hands on others. He was even stealing other people's belongings.

I received phone calls every day or every other day from the school and I'm not exaggerating.

I knew my child was different but I didn't believe he had ADHD. After trying multiple disciplinary techniques nothing was working so I made him an appointment with a therapist. His teachers and I felt that he strongly needed some professional help. His first year in school he was kicked out of school several times and off the bus, and had multiple physical altercations with other children. So I felt forced to take him to the doctor to be diagnosed. I felt like I was neglecting him if I didn't.

I had heard so many horror stories about ADHD medication. I was afraid to give it to my son. But

I felt I was in a position where I had no choice. The teachers were tired and my son was at risk of possibly being expelled. He also wasn't learning anything because he could not focus.

Multiple times I sat outside the door of my son's classroom without him knowing I was there so I could observe his behavior and compare it to other students. I couldn't believe what I was seeing. It was almost as if he had excessive sugar before he entered the class.

There was nothing I could physically do that was helping. This is when I began to pray over my son daily. Then God surrounded my son with wonderful mentors at his school that were willing to give him the attention and extra help that he needed so his life would stay on the right track.

Ms. Deanetris Armstrong became his special education teacher. She went above and beyond the call of duty to make sure my son stayed on track and learned as much as he could. I am forever grateful for this teacher and family friend. I know God sent her to my family's, and many other families' rescue for their children's sake.

Christopher was diagnosed with ADHD and prescribed medication at the age of 7.

The first medication he was given made him act similar to a zombie. He was prescribed the lowest dosage available which was 1 milligram. I still wasn't too happy about giving it to him so I broke the pill in half to make it an even lower dosage. I only gave it to him to make it through the day of school. But he couldn't even make it through school or off the bus or to class because the medication made him so drowsy. There were days I had to carry him and he seemed to have no life in him. I began to get worried; I didn't want the medication to change the good personality that I saw in him or give him side effects in the long run.

The teachers were still calling me not about his extra active behavior but now about how strange he was acting. One day I received a call while I was at work that he would not get up off the floor and was not very responsive. As I rushed to the school to pick him up I walked in the classroom and my son was lying on the floor with 3 to 4 teachers kneeling around him. They described all the abnormal things that he was doing and saying. I knew it was because of the medication-it had him hallucinating.

I took him to the hospital where they checked his vitals, ran some tests and put him in a room for a while. They strongly suggested that I take him back to the doctor and have his medication changed ASAP.

I started doing my own research on ADHD and side effects of the medications.

The school year was ending so I didn't take him back to the doctor to be prescribed anything. I knew my husband and I could manage through the summer with him while school was out.

I can remember every morning was rough in my household. As soon as I woke up I wanted to grab the Excedrin Migraine medication for myself because I knew that the problems my child was going to cause in my household would lead to me having a bad headache.

As my son matured I eliminated as much sugar as I could from his diet. I substituted more fruits and vegetables for the junk food and candy, and whole grain cereals for the sweetened cereals. More physical activity helped him burn energy in a positive way.

Currently he is in middle school and plays the violin. He and his brothers participate in Karate to help with focus, discipline, leadership, and behavior.

At this time the doctor has taking him off of medication. He is receiving one-on-one help in school. Christopher's current teachers have communicated to me that he is well-mannered, courteous, respectful, caring, and kind. He also avoids conflict.

Often our family prays together, and we have family meetings to set goals or discuss issues we may be experiencing. This helps us stay on track.

Having faith in God and taking positive steps have helped us realize that what we went through was only temporary. Although our situations sometime overwhelm us, by making constructive changes we can manage better.

CHAPTER 2

Learn... Understand....Grow

Once you learn the Laws you will experience God's greatness every day of your life. The secrets lie within your heart and are the laws of attraction.

Laws of attraction is the belief that positive or negative thoughts will bring positive or negative experiences into your life. This is one of the most powerful laws in the Universe. If you work to maintain a high frequency through positivity, love, productivity and compassion, you will end up with more goodness in life.

God knew all of us before we were formed in our mothers' wombs. When you speak from your heart you can't go wrong because God lives within in you. Everything you need is inside of you. Sometimes you have to breathe through your heart and realize everything you put out will come back.

The Universe is everything that exists. Karma is a law, not a choice. So give without regrets.

Love unconditionally with a meaning behind it. Speak things into existence. Whatever you want, say it. Know that when you are in alignment, God hears your heart's desires without us even saying a word. Claim things and thank the Universe for it in advance; believe, and know that it's on the way. When your heart is broken, heal it with good thoughts.

Take deep breaths - breathe in the good prana. *Prana* is considered a life-giving force, which is seen as a universal energy flowing in and around the body.   Scream, "It feels so great to be alive!" And tell yourself that you're happy. When you say this it will trigger something in your mind and brain.

When something is good the

brain produces four main feel-good chemicals: endorphin, oxytocin, serotonin, and dopamine.

When something bad is present, you're feeling bad, or in danger the brain produces the chemical cortisol, which is a stress hormone. Too much of this hormone will keep your body at a continuous state of tension. We want moments of happiness and laughter, which are good for the soul and last for a lifetime.

I found myself multitasking daily. My schedule was very hectic and could have been overwhelming if I didn't focus on one thing at a time. A typical day for me normally consists of working 8 hours a day as a sanitation supervisor, carrying a work phone 24 hours a day, parenting 3 children, being a wife, cooking, cleaning, maintaining all the bills, caring for my husband with stage 4 kidney disease, among other obligations to family and friends.

Fully trusting God and understanding how these chemicals affected my body, I learned how to prevent stress, anxiety and depression taking over my life and lived a calm life no matter how massive my daily task or challenges that came my way.

Thankfully there are ways to

increase the happy chemicals in your brain.

1. Coristol = survive then press forward

2. Dopamine = approach and reward

3. Serotonin = be confident and believe in yourself

4. Oxytocin = strengthen trust in yourself consciously

5. Endorphin = make time to laugh

Create happy habits in your

life.

Eat healthier, exercise, get enough rest, listen to music, pray, meditate, and surround yourself with positivity.

CHAPTER 3

Open Our Minds

The good-hearted must remain strong and focus. Some people will hate or dislike you because of their own corrupted past or because of the way others love you. Most humans will eventually let you down. Once you truly understand your purpose in life this gets easier.

Never turn to the evil side even when you are hurting. Deep down in our hearts and souls, we all know that we are God's children; We can choose to follow a good path or a lost path. Ask God to block you from negativity and harm and danger. Ask to be surrounded by goodness and positivity.

Never feel intimidated because there is only one you in the world. Therefore you are special and unique. Know that you are special and no weapon formed against you shall prosper. No matter how strong the hate is continue to press foward. The Universe is working in your favor daily. You can live in harmony and peace.

The enemy can be you and your thoughts and what you inhale and exhale. Only intake what you want to be and create your own reality. Love has no limits. Love can't hurt you unless you allow it to control you. Live a life where time does matter and money is a necessity because you know that they are resources of the earth that flow endlessly. If you are empath, guard yourself.

An *Empath* is someone highly aware of the emotions that surround them. An empathetic person is sensitive to others and has the ability to sense and feel what others are thinking and feeling around them. When you're an empath, you pick up vibrations easier than others.

At the lowest point of your life, you are capable of bringing out the best in yourself.

The pain that afflicted you allows you to dig deep in your soul. You have *Dunimas power* and it lies within you. Activate it!

This is the inner strength, the excellence of soul, that God gave us that doesn't depend on outward things. We are all connected. Live through your heart's desires.

Be pure and wish goodness upon everyone in the world and you will be abundantly blessed. Know who you are and question everything that is set in place, especially from traditions. Don't be afraid to have an open mind and take a risk.

I have learned that the greatest thing in life is love. Multiple things happen in our lives but don't let them make you become numb. Don't let your bones become dry.

Live - Laugh - Love through everything, even the grieving, because everything in this life is God's. God blesses us with it and he takes it away, all in his timing. We must understand that things in life are gifts, including people.

Therefore we should not attach ourselves to anything fully except

God, because one day we must release it. Knowing and accepting this can help us through grieving, losing jobs, or any material possessions.

Changing your mindset and perceptions is a great way to cope with things in life that we have no control over. Once you experience the awakening and you're living in the kingdom, nothing can stop you.

You're on a different level than others on earth. You can experience harmony with peace, and feel it and understand it. Joy will come over you.

Before you know it peace will

come over you and harmony will rule. You will begin to express yourself in a way that words can't. You live through your amazing good thoughts and spirit instead of just speaking them. Remember, actions always speak louder than words. We are what we speak into existence with works and faith.

Be secure and confident in your works. You have the power to heal the world with others as long as your heart has real genuine love. You are capable of the impossible as long as you stay in alignment with God. God will give you the courage to master anything.

The things others take for

granted you will appreciate to the fullest.

The simplest things will bring you happiness because you begin to understand life. Then that's when the simple things become the best things. We no longer label them as simple. A good friend or meal will make you feel complete and healthy. You will realize that good friends are what make you rich. Some people say that money is power, but love rules over all. There were so many things that could have been gone in my life but God's grace allowed me to keep them because I was in alignment and did good deeds with no rejection or hesitation. Don't be afraid to be different, even when people reject you. When I was hurt I still chose to love. I could not help it!

I realize that God created me with a loving heart that could breathe. Everyone is capable of having this but most human beings have let their hearts become numb. Some people have supernatural hearts that forgive and love no matter what. When God speaks to you be open-minded.

Always remember that there's no harm in loving from a distance, if necessary, as long as your heart is pure and you're holding no grudges.

CHAPTER 4

God's Voice

The first time I realized God was speaking to me I cried tears of joy because I knew and understood that it was God. I had been praying for this.

It was a Friday night. I had had a stressful week at work, but not because of the physical part of my job. I was frustrated because management and co-workers seemed to be preoccupied with petty things and had no concept of living in the kingdom.

A few hours after work I went to a restaurant alone. It was very busy, and I was finally seated after a 25-minute wait. After I sat at the table, no waitstaff attended to me and it had been over 30 minutes. I felt very impatient and wanted to leave. But inside my mind I heard a voice speak to me, telling me, "No - do not leave. Someone is coming to pay for your meal."

I said, "Huh? God, is that You speaking to me?"

I immediately looked around the restaurant to see if I knew anyone who would possibly pay for my food. I knew no one. Even so, I felt at peace and I trusted God's voice, because in the prior weeks I had prayed for a gift to know when God was speaking to me. Knowing that I had prayed for this, my heart felt an overflow of love and trust as I sat at the booth for over 30 minutes without being offered a glass of water or anyone taking my order.

At last the waiter approached my table and asked me what I wanted to drink. She didn't apologize or acknowledge my wait. But I remained calm; I never lashed out at her and she walked away to get my glass of water.

As I waited, I recognized a woman entering the restaurant, and realized that I had noticed her in the building where I work. I didn't know her name but I knew she had been diagnosed with cancer. A co-worker had told me this months prior. Although I didn't know her personally, I had prayed for her several times and I felt connected to her.

As she passed my booth I looked up at her and smiled and said hi. She smiled and said hi as her waitress led her to the booth directly behind me. She sat down, then got back up and came to my booth. And said, "We work in the same building, right? I have seen you around."

"Yes, I've seen you too," I replied with a smile. Then she said, "Here - I would like to give you this gift card to pay for your food." My heart fluttered and my stomach had butterflies. I said, "Thank you! That is so nice of you! What is your name?" She told me her name, and asked me for mine. As I told her, I gave her a hug to express my gratitude, then she went back to her booth. By this time tears of joy flowed from my eyes. I said, "Thank you, God! This is one of the best days of my life. You have answered my prayers and have given me understanding and knowledge of what Your voice sounds like inside of me. This is the best gift ever. Now

I know when You are speaking to me. O God, glory to You for this day and this moment! I have never felt so special and happy."

I asked and I received when I was still and in tune. If I had left the restaurant from being impatient or lashed out at the waiter for the long wait I probably would have missed my blessing - not just the gift card but the gift of discernment to know what God sounds like. And also a new friendship with an awesome person who has shared her testimony with me of how she was healed from cancer.

This wonderful lady is now my special friend. We don't talk often but we occasionally cross paths at work. When we see one another we wave and smile and I feel a sensation of peace, wishing that she knew that the way God used her that day changed my life. She holds a special place in my heart.

To remain in alignment you must separate and block all negativity from your life. You must have positive thoughts. Your thoughts are like an invisible wave being released into the atmosphere.

Your heart must wish blessings upon everyone on earth, even if they don't want the best for you. Have faith that every circumstance and trial in your life is working in your favor.

As my husband wrote his first book *I Am Healed Walking In Faith* we were experiencing a foreclosure deadline on our home. Our vehicle was at risk of repossession. But he was in deep alignment so we had no worries. My husband Donald and I learned not to focus on the earthly problems that surrounded us. So as he wrote his book, God supplied all of our needs and more.

He continued to write, even when struggling mentally and physically after being diagnosed with kidney failure and being told to plan his own funeral.

Blessings poured into our home from everywhere even through his heart and soul because he was at a place in his life where he felt strongly connected to all humanity. Though he had gone temporarily blind, he was so grateful that he still had vision in the physical and spiritual form. God heard our hearts' desires in silence because we are connected.

God sent his children who were also in alignment to help us. I received a call from a family member who asked, "Do you need some money?"

I smiled. I knew what was going on - God was sending His

children. Once you have discovered the kingdom you can experience peace, love and joy through anything because you fully know and understand that the battles of life are not yours and you are not alone.

I asked the person on the phone why he wanted to know if I needed money, because I had never revealed any of my financial status to him. He said that we were on his heart and mind. I immediately opened up to him and shared my foreclosure situation. He asked how much more money do you need to end the foreclosure. I hesitated for a moment, then said, "A thousand more dollars."

His response? "When can you come and get it?"

I got in my vehicle and I thanked God the whole way to pick up the money. I promised God that I would share my testimony with others in the world. I also promised God that I would express to the person who offered us the money how he was being used by God to answer my recent prayers that I had released to God, and let go of all worries.

CHAPTER 5

Finish The Race

Focus your life on God, family, and community. Don't put yourself in any uncomfortable or unnecessary financial binds or debts trying to impress or please others. Both material things and immaterial things are only temporary in this life.

Think about it - what can you really say lasts a lifetime? Is there anything that you have owned or possessed since birth? Is there anything that you have used that did not deteriorate or depreciate in value? Do you have any friendships or relationships that didn't get rocky? Once you realize life is precious, you will value it. The good friends in life will help you know your worth and realize what's important.

Your thoughts determine who you are. Most of us are only using a percentage of our brain. Tap in!

I had signed up to be in a race in downtown Flint. I had not prepared for this race other than my daily walking at work or basic physical activities with my sons at home. As over one hundred people stood at the starting line and waited for the "Get on your mark, get set - go!" In my mind and heart I knew I could win even though I hadn't prepared.

Everyone started the 3k race. I kept up with everyone for the first half mile, then I noticed that I was falling behind and getting tired. I began to feel sad and defeated. I wanted to give up. Everyone was passing me and way ahead of me.

But there came a voice in my head that said, "Dont give up, Tiffany! Keep going. Don't focus on anyone or anything around you and know I Am your strength."

I said, "Thank you, God - I hear you!"

I took a deep breath and my second wind kicked in. At that moment in the race it looked like I was almost last. There were very few people behind me. Over half of the walkers were in front of me, but that was no longer my concern. Positive thoughts began to flow through my mind - not of winning, but just finishing the race. The competition was now between me and myself.

My calves started burning, and I realized that I had forgotten to stretch. I was extremely thirsty. I was inhaling and exhaling at a fast pace from my nose and mouth. I had to pull myself together and not focus on what was happening to me as the humidity made sweat roll down my face into my eyes, making them burn. I only had a small distance remaining. I told myself I wasn't giving up.

As I approached the finish line I thanked God for giving me the strength and mind-set to press forward. I thanked God for my five senses and the ability to move all of my limbs to even be a part of the race. I was so grateful.

After everyone finished the race, we entered a small building for race results and a medal and trophy award ceremony.

Even though I knew there were a lot of people who crossed the finish line before me, I still wanted to be a part of the ceremony to congratulate them. As the names were announced I clapped and cheered for everyone, and felt proud of myself for completing the race. Unexpectedly the announcer said, "Tiffany Alston, First Place!" and held up a trophy for me. I looked at my husband because I thought I was hearing them wrong. My husband smiled at me and said, "Go get it."

As I walked down the steps to receive my award, I realized that the greatest reward was the lesson I had just learned from being in the race. No matter what things look like around you or in front of you or behind you, always look up to the hills from where your help cometh. You can't pay attention to what anyone else is doing or how far they are in life or what they have or what they're doing.

Only focus on YOUR goal and never give up, no matter how ugly things look. The other runners were classified in a different age bracket from me; it didn't matter that they were in front of me. So you see, on that day, if I would have let what I saw and the exhaustion I felt steer me into failure, I would not have this awesome story to share with you.

Have you ever accomplished something in life that you didn't even know you were capable of doing or were strong enough physically or mentally to uphold through the task? It's because we are all capable of doing whatever we put our minds to. The more we demand from our inner spirits, the more progress we will get from ourselves. We are all capable of mastering anything when we stay focused and motivated.

As I look at the trophy in my cabinet, I see just a material item. But the lesson behind it fills my heart with joy that I will carry this story throughout my life and share it with others. I knew at that moment that God was giving me a story to share with the world, and I told him I would as I left the race. I pray it will inspire someone to never give up!

Important keys to life consist of putting God first; love, don't hate; give generously; live simply; forgive quickly; be kind. Being committed, open-minded, persistent, thankful, having faith, self-control, and passion are the keys to success.

Sometimes we pray for something and we want it so badly, it can feel painful. It could be something materialistic or it could be a friendship. Once you release it and want it truly in your heart, you will become like a magnet for whatever you release.

You must use your energy and thoughts and words to attract it, and understand the Law to know that to get it you must release it. Yes, I said to get it, RELEASE IT. If you want it fast, instantly RELEASE IT. The more you think about how badly you want it, the harder it is to get it.

It is so possible to love something that you never had before. As human beings we have the ability to look with our physical sight and develop a special emotion in our bodies.

God created us to be so authentic but designed our hearts to love infinitely, even when we are damaged.

Our hearts can be shredded to pieces, yet we still pick them up and carry on through divorces, deaths, abuse, and crises beyond our understanding. The strength of our minds allows us to do this.

As we watch one another, we get stronger and more motivated. The elderly must watch the young, and the young must watch the elderly. They both are wise. My motivation to write this book came from loving unconditionally through life's trials, and overcoming so many obstacles through God's grace.

This has given my life a sense of understanding as to how humans perform. People make us become better versions of ourselves as we watch one another because it's human nature to try to impress one another. Even though we all have flaws we should strive to inspire and perfect.

Sometimes our happiness causes others to build up hatred and envy. This in turn causes distances and separation. Their lives could be different because they are on a lower or higher vibration in life. This could possibly mean that they have not escaped from their negative pasts or are unhappy inside. Their jobs and other people in their lives still have their souls under control. They have not experienced the awakening of knowing what life is really about and what their purpose is.

Never force anyone to experience their awakening; it all comes in stages and as planted seeds grow. Knowledge comes with the lessons in life. Pray for what your heart fully desires, let it go, then endless possibilities will come your way.

If people dislike you or reject you for no reason, this can be normal.

We are all different, and there will always be people who won't get along with us, or who choose to distance themselves from us. Lower vibration people sometimes wear a mask. They are not ready to raise their vibrations; they still have life lessons to learn that you may have already learned. People have fears of being judged or disliked because they are living their lives with a false identity. Instant dislikes can be formed when your own vibrations are clean energy - you are not on the same frequency.

Friends often don't like when your frequency changes so they try to draw you back down; your stillness can be wrongly interpreted. Once you reach higher dimensions, you realize that every day is a beautiful day and every day is a good day as long as you are breathing life. To realize this some people have to go through the worst trials.

ITS ALL ABOUT PERCEPTION. Learning to appreciate life is one of the most happy feelings in the world. You feel amazing inside just because you're present on God's earth and you can interact and connect with others. You can only experience this feeling when you know and understand that life is a gift from our Father, God.

When you're feeling lonely know that our Father God is always present.

God is always surrounding us. God is the Truth, the Light, the Way, the Living Water, the Present, the Future, the Past and Eternity. God will never leave us or forsake us. To find peace we must take our minds off earthly and fleshly things, and let the Universe guide us into greatness because we are fully connected and one with our Creator of heaven and earth. We must have our personal relationship with God.

God will fulfill every void in our lives in His timing.

Times have changed; we are living in a world full of a lot of hurt and bitter and angry people, because they have let the earthly things take over their souls and flesh. If you're not surrounded by positive vibes, this can consume your life and thoughts. Dealing with daily tasks, work, family, etc. can take us to these points of life.

You often see people being less sociable with others because we are scared to be hurt, have trust issues, or we know the world is so competitive and we don't want to compete, so we just stay to ourselves. Once you realize who you are and your purpose, you begin to help others and heal the world with love. Sometimes you have to close your eyes and take deep breaths and know that the more you love regardless of your circumstances the better you will feel.

No matter how great you are everyone will not like you but love anyway and forgive often.

Love the world with your whole heart - even your enemies. If they prey on you, you have nothing to worry about. Just sit back and let God handle their evilness. Karma is one of my only fears in life because I know it's real.

Therefore, I will strive to put nothing but goodness into the world for the rest of the days of my life and I hope you choose to do the same. We are what we believe. Perception is reality. Faith of a mustard seed makes all things possible. Live life fearlessly with no regrets, judgment, or grudges against others and you will be blessed.

CHAPTER 6

Nothing Can Dim Your Light

When your heart is pure and you're in alignment, the sun will beam on you like never before. No one can take away your shine or cover you up because it comes from within you. On a nice sunny day your glow will be so powerful that the rays of the sun will follow you and beam even brighter because you are pure and full of positive energy. No one can take away your light because it's for you. On a beautiful sunny day go outside with no shoes with a clear heart and mind and focus on how grateful you are with a peaceful mind and heart. The sun will find you. The feeling is so great it will overwhelm your soul with joy. You will be happy to have your five senses to experience joy in the Universe.

Plants, animals, insects - all are living things that are connected to the Universe. You will begin to feel connected with them and care for them when they're in harm or danger. You will begin to align your life with the stars. Everything becomes simple and anxiety and depression will not take over you because you have escaped it. You start to experience an awakening and notice things that were always around you but you never paid attention to them. You start to question yourself, asking whether you are just getting older and wiser, or were these things always present in your life and you just didn't recognize them because your mind was asleep and programmed by others and the media?

Spiritual grounding connects our bodies to the earth. Grounding brings physical and emotional balance, and strength. Being grounded helps us react calmly during a crisis. Exercise, salt baths, earth stones, prayer, meditation, good nutrition, spending time in nature, eating pure/raw chocolate, and surrounding ourselves with positive energy helps align our mental and physical state.

Grounding allows us as humans to be at peace and present in our own skin so that we are able to address the issues in our lives.

Ask yourself: Are you woke?

We only get so much time on this earth and should not waste it on things that are meaningless and insufficient. Take the time to pause and free yourself from mental slavery. Bond with yourself and love yourself unconditionally like never before. Close your eyes and go for walks, and talk with God.

Once you get the sensation of gratefulness that takes over your soul and makes you cry tears of joy you have blessings that are on the way. Yes, the journey is so real, and full of heartless people. But one person can change the world and inspire others.

In life we all will experience challenges where we are so weak that we can't lift ourselves back up. This is where we have to be still and don't let pain and evilness regulate our lives. You will doom your soul forever if hurt takes over your mind, body and soul.

Everyone has their own story. Often we cross paths and connect with others that read the story of our lives or listen to us to advise us on our journey. Some of these special people are *lightworkers* who have the ability to know what others think, feel and need to heal.

Once you allow new knowledge in, it can erase the old knowledge and beliefs. Thank God in advance for everything you want to receive, and believe that it is already on the way. If you are in alignment you WILL receive it, so be careful what you ask for and speak. Words are powerful.

There are what seem to be glitches in the system, but it's all part of God's plan. I've been in some situations in my life where God fully took over and intervened. In my mind they were going to head downhill or go wrong because I had no control. But God had a different plan. So I let go of the wheel and let him drive. I literally mean this.

Years ago I was on my way to work on I-475, a curvy highway in Flint, Michigan at about 5:00 a.m. I was driving about 50 mph in fair winter road conditions when a sudden short pour of rain glazed the entire highway for miles with ice. I saw that two cars ahead of me had collided into one another because of the ice. Before I even had the chance to avoid them my car started to spin out of control.

I closed my eyes as my vehicle did over two 360-degree spins. It hit the concrete wall, debris flew all over the highway and my airbag inflated. I could feel the car continue to move a short distance down the freeway before it stopped. I opened my eyes after the impact, held my hands up and said, "God, I'm still alive."

I smiled with the joy of being alive, even though I was so frazzled my body was trembling.

After my car came to a

complete stop I managed to open the door and step out. The expressway was so glazed with ice I fell when my feet hit the ground. I nearly had to crawl across the highway to make it to safe ground.

In the seconds it took to make it to a safe spot on the side of the highway, I heard nothing but loud crashing and saw sparks of fire on the ground and in the air. The next eight cars behind me had crashed, hitting the wall and colliding with other cars. It was like a bad nightmare.

Other people that had crashed and could get out of their vehicles managed their way to the side of the median with me where it was safe.

We shed tears as we thanked God for our lives, even as we could hear others scream in pain while they were trapped in their cars. Conditions were so bad that we could not help get them out of their cars because we didn't know when another car would crash.

Another accident victim and I consoled one another. She was bleeding pretty badly. She had bit her tongue during the accident. We both thanked God for life together that day as we waited for the ambulance. She told me she was on her way to work at the General Motors plant in Willow Run in

Ypsilanti, about 65 miles away. She said that this accident was going to change her life forever.

We both hugged as we cried and again thanked God for life. We said we would never forget that day. We shared all the things we were going to change in our lives from that day forward. We both knew that God had spared our lives and that we were blessed to be alive. As we parted we both felt a special connection with the Universe and one another that I had never felt before.

That day I knew I had experienced God's supernatural intervention. I walked away with only a seatbelt burn on my neck and my car was totaled.

A lady that wasn't involved in the accident stopped to help. She grabbed my hand and asked, "Is that your car over there? God was with you because you're still standing here with me, and you and I both know the impossible has happened today. Let me pray with you."

We both began to say, "Hallelujah! Thank you Jesus! Glory to God!" She said, "Child, go forth this day and walk in your destiny!"

That day I-475 was shut down for miles. There were so many

accidents police and ambulance were delayed for hours. When authorities finally arrived they were from a different county.

Five years after the accident, as I sat at one of my favorite restaurants, Saganos, a Japanese restaurant where you are seated with strangers, as many as 10 at a table. I began to feel like the person next to me wasn't a stranger. I felt like I knew her from somewhere. I glanced at her, not wanting to stare; then I looked at her, deep in her eyes, and the day that we spent together on I-475 instantly flashed through my mind, body and soul. It was the lady who was involved in the crash with me years ago. I told her who I was and she remembered me. We embraced one another with a warm loving hug and a smile. We told each other of all the changes we made in our life since the accident in which others had perished. Both of our relationships with God were solid. We were not only believers but spreaders of his goodness, grace and mercy. I told her I had photos of that day and my husband had made a video of how blessed we were that day. She said she would love to see it. We had an amazing chat and dinner that day.

We exchanged phone numbers and parted ways.

Have you ever experienced deja vu? Or met someone and felt strongly that you had met them before or perhaps you already loved them in your heart deeply? Mysterious things like this happen in life often but it's all part of being one with God.

CHAPTER 7

Some Things Are Divine

I had one of those weeks where even though I was surrounded by hundreds of wonderful people and they loved me, I still felt lonely. My husband had been working 10 hours a day, seven days a week due to mandatory critical plant status at General Motors.

Life sometimes brings married people to feeling lonely because so much of your time is consumed in other things to maintain your lifestyle.

I was having a conversation with a co-worker and we were telling one another how we wanted God to fill the void of loneliness in our lives and how we just needed a good friend who we could trust. After that conversation God spoke to me and said, "Tiffany, be careful what you ask for, because I will give you what you desire."

I asked myself, "Is this what I want? Does my life really need a true friend?"

I have a spouse, and I wouldn't want any friendship to ever affect my marriage, because my husband is my best friend. In my mind I said, yes, God, this is what my heart desires. I want a friend that I can trust around my husband, someone who isn't a user, who loves God as much as I do.

Two days later I woke up on a Sunday morning feeling wonderful. I kissed my husband good morning and gave him some good morning loving, because I knew we wouldn't see one another during the day as he had to get his rest for work.

I showered, and got dressed and debated whether I should pick up some bird food and a few healthy snacks for his lunch.

Feeding the birds was also therapy for me. It gave my heart

peace and I enjoyed watching them. I also felt that God was using me to feed them. It had became a hobby.

I drove to the store to grab a few things out of the food section and headed to the outdoor section for the bird food. On my way I saw a display of newer-style George Foreman grills in the middle of the aisle so I stopped to check it out. As I turned, a young lady was turning from another aisle and we were kind of face to face. It was an old friend from my past who was a true friend during that season of my life. We had lost contact for over 15 years. She was always there for me when I needed anything.

I had often thought of her over the years and even tried to find her for a little while. At the time I was young and I didn't value friendships like I do now. I understand now that real friends are hard to find.

As I looked at her I smiled - my heart was overjoyed. We embraced one another with a warm hug two or three times as we stood in the store and tried to catch up on one another's lives. She said, "This was divined by God for us to meet here today."

I knew that our paths crossing was no coincidence. I was smiling inside because God had told me to be careful what I asked for, and I knew that he had   delivered me my old friend as an express blessing.

We exchanged numbers and addresses and agreed to set up a girls' day out with a lot of time so we could catch up on each others lives.

As I walked away, I said, "I love you, God! You are AWESOME, FAST, and AMAZING."

I knew that God had sent me my friend that I would have for life. I was so excited to see what joy this friendship would bring to my life because I knew it was what my heart fully desired. I already knew that this was no coincidence from that moment we came into one another's presence in the aisle of the store.

Although it saddened me when she told me that her husband had recently died unexpectedly, her sharing that with me and many other personal stories made me appreciate my husband and marriage like never before.

Once again she was a loyal friend. We did not see each other often because of our own family schedules. But we are prayer partners. We pray for one another often. We also send encouraging cards and words of wisdom and family photos through the mail and text often. Just this one connection has changed things for me. It is a good friend that makes you rich, not all the money in the world.

Acquaintances are like a thousand fish in the sea but true friendship should be cherished forever.

CHAPTER 8

Experience An Awakening

I had gone to a higher dimension and was experiencing spirituality daily instead of focusing on religion.

I realize that my husband's health crisis dealing with kidney disease took me to this higher spiritual level. I was thankful and grateful for every moment of life. I was so dependent on God. It's the things in life that challenge you that make you stronger and more successful if you trust God. This helps to have a stronger relationship with God. I Am truly one with God, in alignment, thankful for all my blessings in advance, knowing that no weapon formed against me shall prosper.

If you are in a place in life where you are overwhelmed every day, doing things for others and nothing for yourself, or not spending quality time with God, you need to re-evaluate things. You are in control of your own peace. Take it!

So many people in the world today are having nervous break-downs and anxiety attacks. But they just need to claim their peace that the world has taken away.

Some people don't know how. We have to understand that we are living in a world full of the many unrealistic things that the media presents to us, and people living false lives. We grieve over lost relationships, the loss of jobs, and repossessed items that we can't even take with us once we cross over to the other side.

People feel so much pain and hurt, especially during holiday seasons, mostly because they feel they are missing something that they once had or because they can't afford to make the holiday a materialistic satisfaction for them-selves like they once had before or what they see others doing.

Stop and think: Why should people be sad on holidays because of these things? God has made the day for us and has blessed us with life and breath!

We should be appreciative and thankful and not focused on the man-made holiday that the world has created for celebration. We have to celebrate life every day and the idea that every day is a wonderful day full of endless blessing for our lives.

Be open and willing to let God and His children bring your life JOY and thank him for the amazing gift of discernment. You can sense negativity before it presents itself.

The more I look around, the more the world seems to be designed to make us depressed.

So many people are so concerned with their physical appearance that they are willing to go through unnecessary surgeries and risk dying or causing themselves harm just because they are unsatisfied. They may feel that they have aesthetic flaws because someone else in the world has pointed them out. God did not create everyone the same for a reason.

While surgery for life-threatening problems or birth defects can be necessary, and we should take care of our bodies the best that we can, we should learn to embrace the life that God has given us. We should not worry about aging if we are eating healthy and exercising daily. People fail to realize that worrying makes us age. Worrying can cause stress.

Stress in our lives can cause mental health disorders like anxiety and depression, and heart disease such as heart attacks and abnormal heart patterns, strokes and high blood pressure.

When situations such as

deaths, marriages, financial hard-
ships, divorces, illness, job loss,
etc., occur, we need to monitor
ourselves, because stress can kill
you.

By knowing about the three
different types of stress (acute,
episodic acute and chronic), I
learned coping strategies that
allowed me to take control. I
managed my time better, got more
sleep, did more physical activity,
talked with a friend, meditated and
prayed, read a book, went for nature
walks, and learned to say no.

I focused on one situation at a
time, so that my mind was not
overwhelmed, regardless of how

many things were coming at me at one time.

I often felt that in order for me to have peace, I had to be alone. There were some days I had to zone out and listen to music that made me happy. This was therapy for me and good for my soul. The music I listened to had no words so I created my own.

As I sat outside surrounded by nature and wrote this book, I found that writing was my therapy, too.

Nothing in life stays the same - things are always changing like the weather, including friends, jobs, spouses, children, living locations, life skills, knowledge and wisdom.

Once you learn this, nothing will get you down for too long because you understand that it was just a storm passing through, and you can share your experience to help someone else in this life. When you help others and put out good energy it will always come back to you. I realize that I had been doing this my whole life and this is part of the reason I'm so blessed and happy.

There is an endless field of positive energy that is surrounding me and it's getting larger every day. I Am spreading more goodness and love into the Universe.

I Am walking in my destiny.

This field of energy is so powerful that people with negative energy stay away from me even when I was weak and willing to allow it in. It was blocked.

Repeat this daily:

I Am healthy

I Am grateful

I Am love

I Am joy

I Am bold

I Am wealthy

I Am beautiful

I Am confident

I Am God's Masterpiece

And So Are You!

If another human being continues to hurt you, don't be afraid to cut them loose ASAP. There may be a time in life where you can rekindle things but at that moment you have no time to waste when there are endless possibilities in the world with others who won't hold you back and will push you forward into your purpose.

So many people are afraid to move forward because they feel they have no one. This leaves them to wallowing in misery and never moving forward.

We see this so often but all we can do is plant a seed in them and let them allow the Universe to let it blossom or, if they're around us long enough, water it with wisdom, knowledge and love.

Real beauty is someone's heart and how it loves and heals others. Sometimes the people we want in our life are not meant for us. We often spend lots of time and energy focused on them, trying to love them or get them to notice or appreciate us when they don't want our love and could care less if we even existed. We can't focus our thoughts on this; it causes us to become hurt and bitter and feel worthless and sad from rejection when the timing is just not right or may never be. So just move on.

If for some reason you are surrounded by them because they are your neighbors, co-workers, or family members, just know that they're probably there as a learning experience for you, or for you to be a positive example to them. As they watch you from the sideline, they are learning from you.

That higher power is saying that they can't be in your life fully because you will clash. You're not on the same page. They may put your life a few chapters ahead or behind; everything is in God's timing.

When we are not in alignment, we go off on our timing and get off course. If you take the time to be still and meditate, things in your life will fall into place. The things that you leave behind will unblock you from going to the next level. Are you seeing the light or are you still in the dark?

Experience an awakening of an unprogrammed mind.

Be willing to do your own research on everything you have been told or taught in this life including religion and spirituality.

Religion is a particular system

of faith or worship, with rituals or beliefs.

With spirituality we search in our hearts and souls for something beyond the physical world. Believe it or not, we are capable of so many things and we are experiencing so many things that most of us don't understand. Don't be afraid to use the technology that we now have to get answers.

There are multiple sources to receive clarity, including books, the internet, the study of different cultures, classes in theology, human experience and more.

Too often, humans judge a

culture or a group of people based on appearances alone. While their customs may seem strange to us, remember that there are reasons behind their actions.

Most people won't even take the time to research these reasons, even though another human being sacrificed time in their life to write the books so we could learn about them.

It has been said that knowledge is power.

The knowledge that we can acquire can make our journey easier, because we can learn something from the experience and knowledge of others, so that we wouldn't have to go through it.

CHAPTER 9

The Beauty Of Life

Life becomes even more beautiful once you realize you are your own movie. You choose whether it is Fiction or Nonfiction; a thriller, horror, drama, love, or simple story.

There are several dimensions to life. Just as in a video game, you must be in tune and a different character to enter each one.

When they tell us in school we can be whatever we want to be there is truth behind it. But most people don't look at the depth of the meaning. Create your own reality.

Regardless of our environment, we choose what we put in it. Even if we have a horrible job, if we change our mindset we can see it as greatness.

Changes can start with manifestation. *Manifestation* is the outward display of emotion or feeling, or something theoretical coming into actual existence. With the power of manifestation, you can make your vision become reality.

The things we want in the Universe are already ours. With clear thoughts and thinking on the matter, the manifestation will take place.

When I decided to just live in the moment things were marvelous in my life.

I stopped the planning and other than my job, time had stopped for ME.

I no longer saw time as twelve-thirty. I saw it as one-two-three-zero. I stopped seeing death as a depressing thing and I looked at it as a new journey. The thought of death made me appreciate my own life and value all the good people I had in my life.

I woke up daily with a smile,

wondering what God had planned for me, knowing that blessings were coming my way, even if it was a kind word that would warm my heart or give my soul joy.

The more I looked at the sky the more beautiful things I saw. Some weeks I saw a rainbow almost every day. Some days the clouds were rainbow clouds. The earth was beginning to look like what I thought was a small glimpse of heaven on earth.

I watch others who never take the time to enjoy it and give their minds peace and harmony. It's actually therapy without a doctor and medicine. Having three kids, working full time, and having a spouse with stage 4 kidney disease, I needed this therapy and God supplied it.

On the real special days, regardless of the season, God allows the Sun to beam on me in a special way; when It hit me it would beam even brighter. If it was behind the clouds it found me. This had probably been happening my whole life but I never took the time to focus on it and pay attention.

I began to watch birds snatch bugs out of the air and eat them. I began to see that the rabbits, squirrels and birds were friends and could sit next to one another and enjoy a meal. But there were some kinds of birds that were not allowed in or came to destroy the feast, just as all humans can't break bread together.

I noticed that not just nocturnal animals came out at night. Some of the more gentle animals came out and took the risk of getting eaten alive. Animals' lives are so similar to ours, but they have their own language and habitats.

I had sat on my screened porch on several occasions, but for the first time I noticed that nighttime was not silent. It was actually noisier than the average spring morning. It was full of noises I had never heard and could not make out what they were.

You have to test this out for yourself on summer nights outside in a safe place. Count the number of different sounds you can hear. This was my night therapy. It even sharpened my mind.

I started to realize that everything was a repeat. We were all just doing the same thing over and over.

When someone came up with something that was kind of new, such as an invention, or found something to make life easier, they were praised or it was announced to the world. If you announced it too fast without proper legalization or rights, someone in the world would steal your idea for themselves. And if you didn't act on an idea or creation fast enough you would have regrets because someone stole your idea without you even telling them.

Because we are all connected, dealing with similar things in life, this can cause different people to think of some of the same creations to simplify life or help us be happier.

If you are a focused, motivated individual, you know how powerful thoughts and ideas are; you will begin to make them into blueprints and brain- storming charts, so that the manifestation of the idea can start and be released into the atmosphere.

CHAPTER 10

The Journey of Faith

Meditation and prayer are so powerful. Meditation is an approach which focuses and clears one's mind in order to attain emotional and mental calmness. Prayer is our spiritual communication with God.

I had prayed my whole life and yes, it was effective. But once I combined prayer and meditation my results were mind-blowing. It became addictive, and was so effective that my life was never going to go without them both.

I knew the power that was within them both. I had experienced it.

When a challenge arose in my life I didn't look at it as a challenge. I looked at it as an experience. I learned not to pray and meditate on worries and problems themselves, but to meditate on the results that I wanted and envision them.

Once you learn to follow your heart the Universe starts to reveal the truth of life and who you really are. We have to focus ourselves on love, truth, unity, family, health, and humility; then we can be who God created us to be in this life regardless of our circumstances.

Start using your intuition to find more genuine happiness and peace.

Healing power lies within anyone who believes they possess it, and practices it.

There are keys and secrets that lie within the Scriptures.

The moment I stopped valuing money for the things we think we need it for was one the best days of my life.

I began to work in the Universe as one with God. No matter what another human being saw as a struggle, it wasn't for me. It was a chance for me to increase my faith and continue to bless others and watch what amazing things were continuously happening in my life.

There were days that I had less than fifty dollars to my name, but I had to release and bless someone else with it because I had to follow my heart.

There were days God spoke to me and I had to lay money on the floor of a restaurant restroom for a person I would never know to enter and pick it up.

Before leaving I wrote "God Bless" in soap on the mirror. But it was my assignment from God. The more I did, the more I was blessed with not just material things and money but with the power of healing, of feeling whole and loved almost beyond what I could handle.

I no longer cared what others thought of me - I had accepted my purpose in life and I was enjoying the amazing journey.

The less I cared about money the more it came.

Some days I just looked on the ground and there were twenty dollar bills in front of me. I knew it was only God supplying my every need.

Life brought me to a point

where I only cried out in confidence and I only feared Karma. I was so connected, I dreaded to hurt anyone because I knew what would be in store for me. So with everyone that surrounded me, I had to love them well from the heart, or separate myself from them. I understood that my blessings were based upon how I treated others.

The more good I did the more love God showed me, whether it was a new job offer, a paid-off bill, a new friend, a free meal, or beauty in the sky. I was amazed - I knew I was God's masterpiece.

Never worry if you believe and trust that God already has it figured out. Some of my prayers and heart's concerns have been answered in ways and conditions I never would have imagined or dreamed of. This concept may be too complex for any of us to understand. While we are stuck trying to figure out how it could work it's already done. Once you accept this you have power and joy and the truth lies in you and it will set you free.

I have an awesome relationship with God. I am happy inside because of this. He answers all of my heart's desires. Even if I speak with my heart and not with my mouth, God hears me. I know I am His child so I don't need to worry.

And I love the journey!

It is full of greatness and the revelation of surprises beyond our understanding. You can go where you wanna go and be who you wanna be.

My suggestion to the world is just don't waste time - it is so precious. Live in a mindset where a minute is a day and a month is a year.

Accept responsibility for your own actions and stop blaming.

This is so powerful and it gives US power. When you put blame on others, it takes your power away.

Never blame anything on Satan. Don't give him any credit for anything.

If something happens in your life that you disagree with, just accept it, take control and change it. Know and understand who you are and WHOSE you are - the child of the Creator, the King of everything that exists.

There's nothing wrong with starting over. We learn as we go through the lessons of life. We learn not to make the same mistake multiple times.

Some mistakes are good and should not be labeled as failure

because they take us into some of the most prosperous times of our lives.

When we say "I do," do we really know what we are committing our lives to? Do we really know what lies ahead of us? Do we really know what we must endure?

I want you to know what this truly means. My husband and I are experiencing the "In sickness and in health til death do us part" portion of our vows. And through it all, we must remember to keep the faith.

I thank God for my family's second chance. I thank God for giving my husband a new life, a new beginning with dialysis. We are walking out our destiny for ourselves, living for God, imperfect but striving for perfection in a world of temptation.

God will never put more on us than we can bear, even in our relationships. He cares for and loves us, both individually and together. You must endure to the end even through sickness and health.

When my husband found out that his kidneys were failing, we knew that we had to take our marriage and prayer life to a different level together to survive. He had always had been good to me throughout our marriage; I loved

God and believed in being one with my spouse, so I knew that I was in it for the long haul - til death do us part, as I said during my vows. It was almost as if I was a single mother for months. We were low on cash; often bills were delinquent. But nothing mattered except his life.

We no longer cared about holidays, gifts, cars, etc. We had to focus on our faith and his healing. He had multiple hospitalizations that were two weeks long and he went temporarily blind.

My perception of him starting dialysis was a new journey with God allowing me to still have him as a gift in life. When others thought of it as the end stage, it was our new beginning to make a difference in others' lives through knowledge, love, and connecting with others.

My children and I had held hands and prayed together multiple times.

Prayers are so powerful when two or more come together, know and believe anything can come to pass.

It doesn't matter if it is impossible - there is nothing that is too hard for God. God always has that ram in the bush, even if it's been on fire.

Activate your faith and know

that you are God's masterpiece. Hallelujah!

In this life we must make the best of whatever we have, because the scriptures say everything is working together for our good. Throughout this life I have been through numerous things.

I grew up in a home that society would call broken (parents divorced), have a spouse with end-stage kidney failure, have been passionate for people who had no love for me, experienced foreclosure twice as an adult, went through bankruptcy around the age of 30, had an unplanned pregnancy that resulted in triplets with only one infant fully developing and surviving, had surgery in my 20s for mild dysplasia (pre-cancerous cells around the cervix wall), lost loved ones, had a child with ADHD, had a vehicle in risk of repossession, had serious thoughts of the circle of life stages going through my mind as a young adult, felt deep disappointment in some local religious organizations, experienced the rejection and loss of friends because I loved God and was different. I hit rock bottom more than once.

All I can say now is thank you, God! You brought me through, you brought me OUT. I'm living through you and you're living within me so I can share my testimonies with others of how I made it, how I was still allowing you to work miracles in my life. But I understand that life is what you make it.

No matter the environment you come from or circumstances, your destiny depends on you, your faith and trust in God.

Many people dwell on their present circumstances or get stuck in the present time. Don't get held back from becoming your best YOU. Life may give us bitter lemons but we can make them into sweet lemonade. Life may detour us but we can get back on the right road.

It's never too late to start over.

We are never too old for a new beginning.

Understand that everything you have been through this far has happened for you to become that great version of you to succeed and help bless others.

I Am healthy

I Am wealthy

I Am love

I Am joy

I Am grateful

I Am   bold

I Am confident

I Am beautiful

I Am God's Masterpiece

And So Are You!

EPILOGUE

To be continued in the next book.

I will have a remarkable testimony of my family's new journey that God will bless us with. I am thanking God in advance for either full restoration of my husband's kidneys or a transplant.

SUPPORTIVE SCRIPTURES

1 Corinthians 16:14
Do everything in love.

Proverbs 12:25
Anxiety in a man's heart weighs him down, but a good word makes him glad.

Proverbs 23:7
As a man thinks in his heart, so is he.

1 Peter 5:7
Cast all your anxiety on him because he cares for you.

Philippians 4:6-7
Do not be anxious about anything, but in everything by prayer and supplication with thanksgiving let your request be known to God.

Deuteronomy 31:8

It is the Lord who goes before you. He will be with you; he will not leave you nor forsake you. Do not fear or be dismayed.

Isaiah 26:3

You will keep him in perfect peace, Whose mind is stayed on You, Because he trusts in You.

Matthew 7:7-8

Ask, and it shall be given to you; seek, and ye shall find; knock, and it shall be opened unto you. For every one that asketh receiveth; and he that seeketh.

Matthew 9:29

According to your faith, shall it be done to you.

Matthew 21:22

And whatever things you ask in prayer believing, you will receive.

Romans 12:2

Do not conform to the pattern of this world, but be transformed, by the renewing of your mind.

CONTACT INFORMATION

To contact the author, or if you are interested in being a living kidney donor for Donald Alston:

Email: walkinginfaith111@gmail.com

Email: tiff5907@gmail.com

Facebook: Walkinginfaith111

9 781734 086539